Dd E

Jj Kk Ll

Pp Qq Rr

Vv Ww Xx

abc
for adults

TOBY LEIGH

Adult learning is vital

Children's ABC books in the 1970s taught us about a warm and innocent world through the wonderful hand-painted imagery of animals, toys and quaint household objects. Unfortunately, we all grew up and became paranoid, cynical adults unable to cope with the world around us. But don't despair, this new book will help guide you and your family through this difficult phase of your existence.

By learning the simple words in this book, you will gain an excellent grasp of how terrifying adult life can be. It is recommended that you read and practice these words as often as possible in order to nurture a well-formed pessimistic outlook.

The bold and friendly illustrations have been designed to help even the most jovial adult recognise the hatred and fear that resides within them.

The vocabulary found in the book is recommended for adults between the ages 25 - 100.

This book belongs to:

Toby Leigh, the author of ABC for Adults is himself an experienced and paranoid adult. He was also once a smiling child with a yearning for knowledge. Further cynical material by the author can be found at **www.tobyleigh.com**.

apple

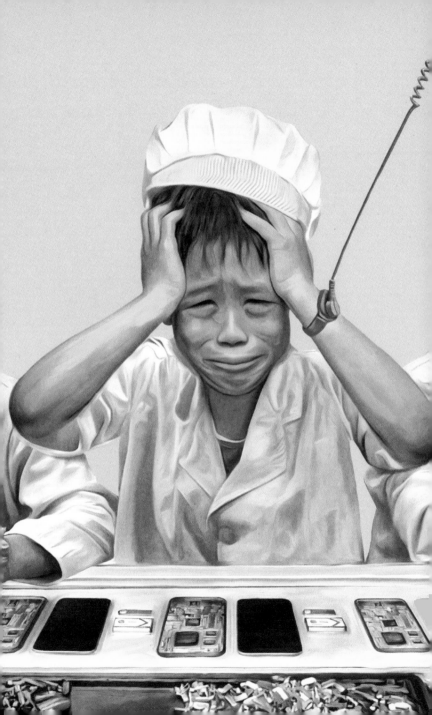

box

C

computer

dog

egg

fox

girl

heart

i

insect

jacket

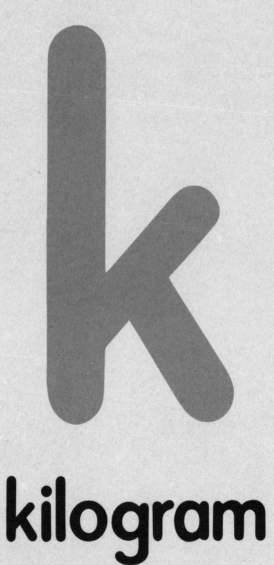

kilogram

lamb

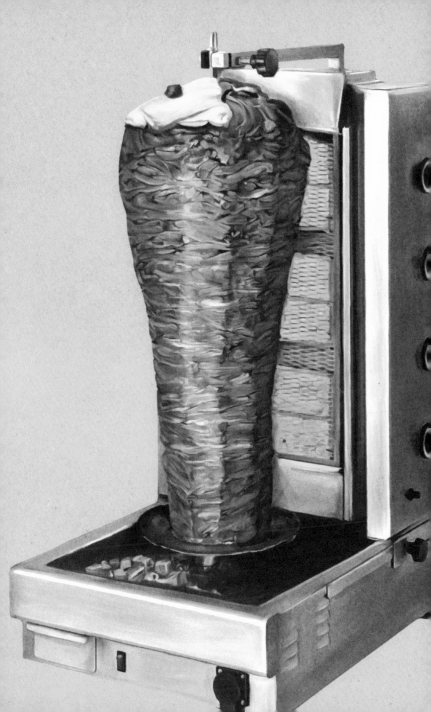

mouse

nose

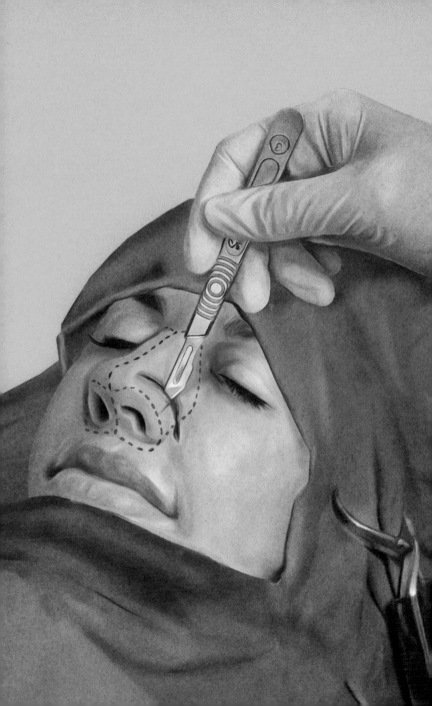

orange

policeman

queen

rhinoceros

soldier

tongue

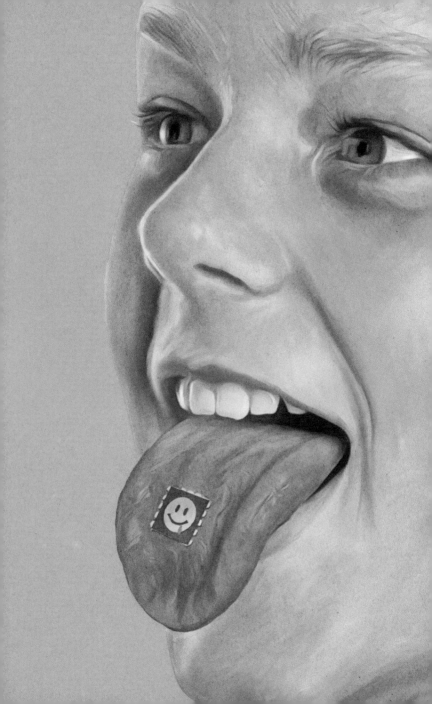

uniform

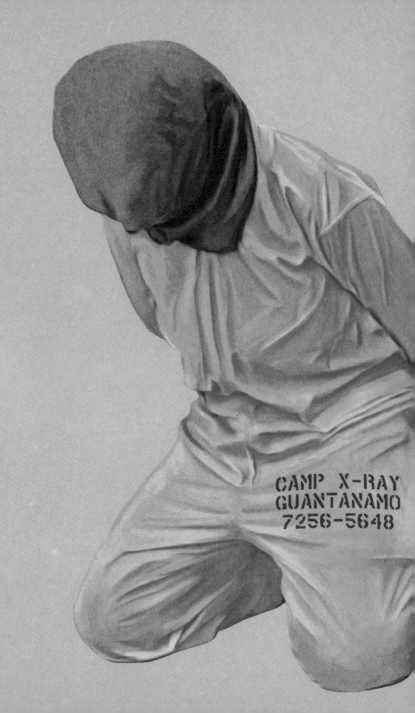

vest

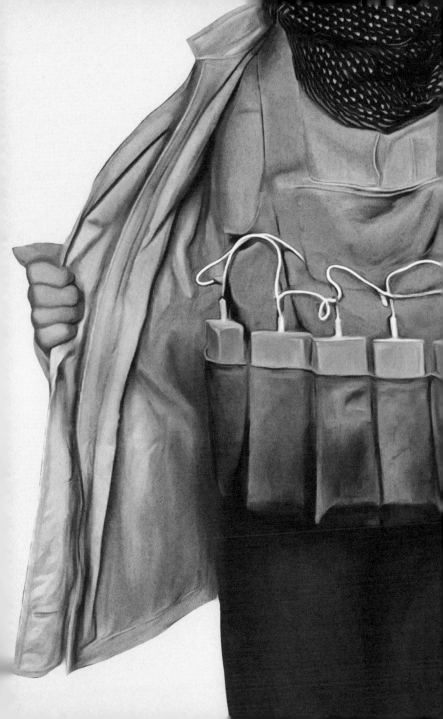

whale

x-ray

yacht

Z

zip

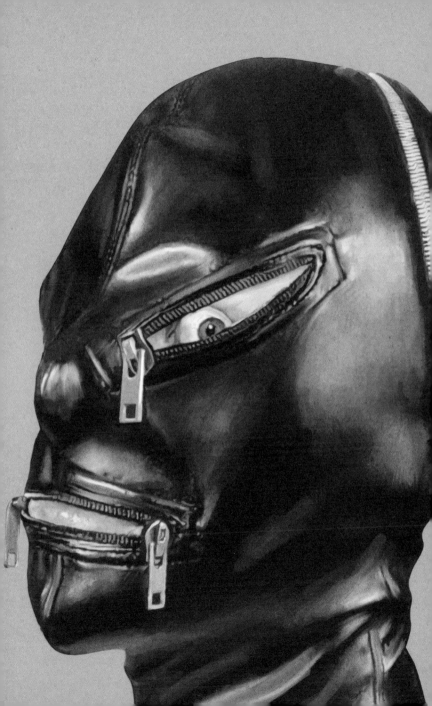

Thanks to:

Clive Francis
Matthew Murdoch
Jack McGinity
Michael Glickman
Allan Corduner
Omid Asghari
Mark Carter
Averil Sinnott
Graham Griffiths
Andrew Murphy
Philip Jackson
Sam Blair
Hugo Weinberg
Joe Blair
Marlene Sidaway
Marina Carter
Chris Stott
Eloise Moody
Philip Currie
Olney Atwell
Danny Flint
Phil Lee
William Stein
Nicholas Dawe
Elsie Bryant
Ellie Jacob
Alastair Scott
Louisa Steyaert
Alison Steadman
Jean-Louis Schuller
Lesley Manville
Israel Hurtado Cola
Phil Reeves
Jamie Barnes
Richard Gay
Damien Irving
Tom Ludgrove
Chris Jack
Ruth Sheen
Will Tyler
Colin and Gill Cina
Jethro Aukin
Kerry Keays
Michael Weller
Jemima Berridge
Graham Robson
Laurie Britton Newell
Michael Ainsley
Mark Cocksedge
Suzanne Azzopardi

Sally Hawkins
Piers Ridyard
Tom Cohen
Eleni Leoussi
Shamir Sidhu
Matt Clarke
Gemma Loughran
Sam Coulby
Alex Ramzy
Sandra Ahn Mode
Jonathan Garelick
Paul Levy
Alexander Lehmann
Les Blair
Sarah Harvey
Jason Ahn
Ben Freeman
Ewan Flynn
João Branco
Rich Woods
Jeannette Murphy
Zac Chapman
Paul Cocksedge
Angelique Ello
Matthias Hoene
Jack Trench
Karen Cattini
Alice Bailey johnson
Oren Laufer
Matthew Maran
Caroline Leleux
Kim Thome
Marilyn Jacobson
Nick Bradley
Meryl Fernandes
Katherine MacEwen
Joanne Mitchell
Miles Maynard
Renato Lopes
Alasdair Dixon
Jonathan Jacobson
Tom Edmunds
John Hardiman
Christian Nolle
Chris Davie
Adam Farlie
Stan Chow
Luke Blair
Jonathan Chamberlain
Jesse Richards

Christoph Bolten
Jitesh Patel
Leo Leigh
Heather Ring
Debbie Kilbride
William Mosse
Dan Gasper
Chris Bradbury
Faye E J Ward
Daniel Jacobson
Jack Trench
Andrew Morgan
Ray Harvey
Charlie Smith
Angel Coulby
Georgina Lowe
John Hannah
Ali Collins
Aron Fish
Lucinda O'reilly
Colin Jones
Lucy Tauber
Anna Trench
Lexi Whiteford
Steve Baker
Anthony Ellis
Dave Turbitt
Marion Bailey
Andrew Lavin
Romain Forquy
David Horovitch
Anthony Holt
Michael Elwyn
Toby Kress
Jo Biddiscombe
Andrew Walker
Jonathan Harvey
Joseph Oakley
Caroline Harvey
Hip-Hopbackintheday
Liam Dystant
Greg Martin
Gareth Holt
Tom Fletcher
Emma Lacey
Danny Flynn
Matt Smith
Billy Elliott
Anna Skrein
Kate Church

© Toby Leigh 2018
ISBN : 978-1-5272-2419-3

Aa Bb Cc

Gg Hh Ii

Mm Nn Oo

Ss Tt Uu

Yy Zz